# TRADITIONAL TALES
*from*
# CELTIC
# LANDS

Vic Parker

Based on myths and legends retold by
Philip Ardagh

Illustrated by
Stephen May

Chrysalis Children's Books

First published in the UK in 2000 by

(c) Chrysalis Children's Books

An imprint of Chrysalis Books Group Plc

The Chrysalis Building, Bramley Road, London W10 6SP

Paperback edition first published in 2004

ISBN 1 84138 126 8 (hb)

ISBN 1 84138 948 X (pb)

British Library Cataloguing in Publication Data
for this book is available from the British Library.

Editor: Stephanie Turnbull

Designer: Zoë Quayle

Educational consultant: Margaret Bellwood

Printed in China

# CONTENTS

# The Celtic Lands

**The stories in this book were first told by the Celtic peoples.
These folk lived more than a thousand years ago in the countries
that today we call Scotland, Ireland, Wales and England.
Celts also lived in the northern part of France we call Brittany.**

Long, long ago, the Celtic lands were covered with thick green forest.
Misty mountains towered over unexplored valleys and thundering
waterfalls swirled into mighty rivers. The islands were surrounded
by stormy seas that crashed on to their rocky coastlines. Brave warrior
tribes lived on these islands. Each tribe was led by a fierce chieftain
and the chieftains were ruled by kings. The kings lived in huge castles
that were big and strong enough to keep out invaders.

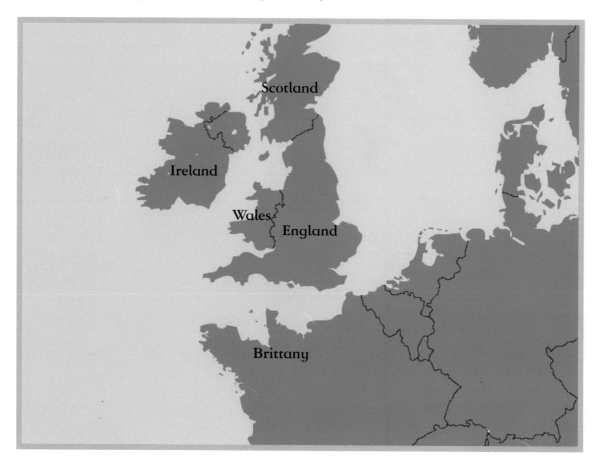

**Celtic stories are full of magic and mystery.
They tell of heroes with superhuman skills,
sorcerers who weave strange spells and
faeries who make mischief wherever they go.**

The Celts didn't write down their stories. The tales were told out loud by poets. The poets travelled around from village to village, entertaining tribes with the deeds of heroes and villains. This is how the stories spread all over the Celtic lands.

Over the years, the tales grew and changed. Stories that are now about different people and places might once have been about the same hero or event. For example, some experts think that the Welsh character Llew and the Irish character Lug are the same person.

*This cup was crafted by Celts over
1,000 years ago. It is made of silver.*

# THE BLACKSMITH'S BOY

There was once a little island that lay far off the western
coast of Scotland. The island was often hidden by mists
of sea-spray and clouds of fog. Many people who lived
there thought that it was a place of magic. They said
that faeries, or Little People, lived near the village in
a small, smooth, round hill called Green Knoll. The
villagers believed that on nights when there was a full
moon, a secret door appeared in the knoll. The Little
People crept out and ran off to the village to make
mischief. They hurried back inside the knoll before the
dawn, when the door mysteriously disappeared.

Many villagers had searched for the hidden entrance
to the knoll, but no one had ever found it. Several folk
were sure that they had heard hammering coming from
deep inside and they thought that the Little People must
be busy beating hot metal into mighty weapons.

Other people thought such reports were nonsense.

'Iain the blacksmith lives near to Green Knoll,' they
scoffed. 'It's just the sounds from his smithy.'

But Iain himself had heard the muffled, clanging
noises that came from somewhere deep underground.

Iain was sure that there were Little People living inside Green Knoll and he also believed that their magic had been at work in his own home. Iain was a hardworking man, but his son was extremely lazy. Each day, while Iain sweated in his hot smithy, the child just lay in bed. No matter how much the boy ate and drank, he always stayed as thin as a beanstalk. Iain suspected that there was something strange about this...

One night, when Iain was having supper at a farmer's house, he decided to tell his friends about his fears.

'I'm worried that my boy isn't what he seems,' he began. 'I think that the Little People took my child away to Green Knoll and replaced him with a faery child disguised as my son.'

'You mean, your boy is a changeling?' gasped the farmer.

'I think so,' sighed Iain. 'But how can I be sure? And if I'm right, how can I get rid of the changeling and rescue my real son?'

'Hmmm,' said the farmer's wife. 'I've heard that if a changeling sees something truly extraordinary, he forgets his disguise and cries out in his true voice.'

Iain shook his head sadly.

'But I have nothing extraordinary to show him,' he sighed unhappily.

The friends jumped as the door of the farmhouse suddenly blew open and an old man hobbled in.

'Iain,' said the mysterious guest, 'here's what you must do...'

The surprised blacksmith listened carefully to every word the strange old man said.

The next day, when the boy demanded a drink, Iain followed the old man's instructions. He took the child two tiny eggshells filled with water, but pretended that they were as heavy as huge kegs of beer. Iain staggered into the child's bedroom, huffing and puffing with each step.

The amazed boy let out an evil cackle and cried in a gruff, croaky voice, 'I've never seen anything like that!'

Iain now knew for sure the boy was a changeling, but he didn't say a word. Instead, he calmly began to add logs to the fire. The flames roared higher and higher. All at once, Iain grabbed the child and flung him towards the blaze. Quick as a flash, the changeling flew up into the air, burst through the roof and disappeared forever.

Iain was very relieved. Now all he had to do was get his real son back. Luckily, that very night there would be a full moon. The entrance to the Green Knoll would appear. It was time to put the second part of the old man's plan into action...

As soon as darkness fell, Iain put a Bible in his pocket and hid a cockerel under his coat. Then he tiptoed silently to the grassy mound. Sure enough, a pale door shimmered in the silver moonlight. Nervously, Iain pushed it. The magical entrance swung open. There before him lay a long, murky tunnel.

Iain took a deep breath and stepped into the gloom. He stumbled forward along the cold, damp passage. As he went deeper underground, the tunnel became lighter and lighter. A warm orange glow began to flicker upon the walls. Clank... clank... clank... came the sound of hammering, growing louder all the time. The tunnel became hotter and hotter.

At last the tunnel opened out into a huge hall. There were Little People scurrying everywhere. Some were stoking a blazing fire. Others were carrying tools and metal. More were running about with buckets of steaming water. Towering above them all was a human boy, hard at work hammering hot metal.

'My son!' gasped Iain, bravely holding out his Bible as protection against the faeries' magic.

The Little People heard Iain gasp and turned to face him in surprise. They were so stunned that they didn't notice Iain slip the cockerel out from under his coat.

But they all heard the startled cockerel cry out,
   'Cock-a-doodle-doo!'
   'The dawn!' the Little People cried in terror. They
thought that the secret door was about to disappear –
and some of their friends were still away making mischief
in the village. The latecomers would be locked outside
the Green Knoll until the next full moon!
   As the Little People ran to and fro in panic, Iain
snatched his son and ran for his life, back up the long
tunnel and out of the magical door into the moonlight.
By the time the faeries realized they had been tricked,
the overjoyed blacksmith and his boy were safely back
at home where they belonged.

# THE BRIGHT ONE

Gwydion was a man with magical powers. These mysterious skills had been given to him by his uncle, Math, the greatest sorcerer in the whole of Wales.

Gwydion once cast a spell on a beautiful woman called Arianrod to make her give birth to his son. Gwydion knew that Arianrod wouldn't be at all pleased about it, so he made his magic so strong that Arianrod didn't even know she'd had the child.

Gwydion smuggled the baby away and brought him up on his own. The boy grew up fair and strong and clever and Gwydion was very proud of him.

'What a shame that Arianrod doesn't know about her son,' Gwydion often thought. 'I'm sure she'd love him as much as I do. Maybe I should tell her, after all...'

On the child's fourth birthday, Gwydion made up his mind. He took his son to Arianrod's lonely castle by the sea. The child stood at the windows of the great hall while his father and Arianrod talked together in whispers. Suddenly Arianrod let out a shrill cry.

'I have a son?' she screamed. 'Gwydion, how dare you trick me!'

Arianrod stared hard at the boy. He looked back at her with her own steady gaze and she knew it was true.

'What is his name?' Arianrod asked, in a low voice.

'He has no name,' Gwydion explained. 'I thought it only right that his mother should choose it.'

'Then he will stay nameless forever!' Arianrod cried. 'I shall never forgive you, Gwydion!'

She strode away, her cloak billowing behind her.

'I swear I will make you name our son!' Gwydion shouted after her.

Furious, Gwydion marched down to the seashore with the child. He murmured words of magic as he went. As the spell began to weave its enchantment, Gwydion and his son began to change into the form of a shoemaker and his young helper...

Arianrod soon heard that an expert shoemaker was busy at work on the beach. She hurried to the shore and asked him to make her a pair of beautiful new slippers.

While the shoemaker measured and hammered and sewed, Arianrod watched his young helper shooting birds with his bow and arrows. The child didn't miss a single shot. Bird after bird tumbled out of the skies. Finally the boy took aim at a tiny wren. It flew so high that it was no more than a speeding black dot.

The golden-haired boy shot the arrow and the wren fell on to the sand with a soft thud.

'Oh, well done!' Arianrod laughed, clapping her hands. She turned to the shoemaker. 'The bright one has a steady hand. What is his name?'

'You have just given him one,' cried the shoemaker with glee. 'It is Llew Llaw Gyffes, which means The Bright One, or the Lion, with a Steady Hand.'

Arianrod's eyes flashed fire as the magic melted away and she saw who the shoemaker and his helper really were.

'Aren't you proud of your son?' Gwydion urged. 'He's sure to become a fine warrior one day.'

Arianrod felt nothing except rage at Gwydion's trick.

'Llew will never become a warrior,' she cursed. 'For I swear that he will not have armour nor weapons unless I give them to him – and I never will!'

With that, Arianrod stormed back to her castle. She barred the gates and did her best to forget all about Gwydion and her son.

Several years later, Arianrod welcomed two wandering poets into her castle to entertain her guests at a feast. Little did she know that the two poets were really Gwydion and her son, magically disguised once again. By this time, Llew had grown into a brave young man.

Gwydion was determined to make Arianrod somehow give her son armour and a sword, so he could win honour and glory as a warrior.

That night, while everyone snored in their beds, Gwydion crept to the top of the castle and whispered magical and mysterious words out over the sea. When the sun rose next morning, Arianrod's guards saw a terrible sight – a whole fleet of enemy ships waiting to attack! The guards raised the alarm at once and soon everyone was armed and ready to defend the castle.

'Please stand and fight with us,' Arianrod begged the two poets. She quickly buckled armour on to the younger man and handed him a pile of weapons. The very moment she did so, the fleet of enemy ships faded away to glimmers of sunlight on the water and the two poets changed back to their true selves. Llew stood strong and proud in his new armour. He was now a true warrior.

Arianrod trembled with rage at being tricked yet again. She was determined to have her revenge.

'I swear that there is not, never was and never shall be, a woman from any of the races in the world who will take Llew as her husband,' she screamed.

It was a terrible curse. Arianrod had chosen her words cleverly. She was sure that now Llew would never marry.

But Arianrod had forgotten about Gwydion's uncle, the mighty magician Math. The famous sorcerer was happy to help Gwydion. He used powerful magic to weave together thousands of sweet-smelling flower petals into a woman who was as lovely as nature itself.

'Her name is Blodeuwedd, which means Flower Face,' Math told the overjoyed Llew. 'She has not been born of any of the races in the world and so she can be your bride.'

Llew and Blodeuwedd were married at once. As a wedding gift, Math gave them lands to rule over in the hills of Ardudwy. Llew lived there with Blodeuwedd for many happy years, ruling well and wisely over his people.

# THE MASTER OF MASTERS

There were many mighty castles in Ireland, but by far
the greatest was the castle of Tara. It was the home of
the High King of all Ireland.

One wild and stormy night, a royal messenger came
galloping to Tara as fast as he could. He flung himself
off his horse and thumped hard on the gates.

'Let me in!' he bellowed. 'I have an urgent message
for the High King.'

The news was very bad. The giants across the sea
were preparing to attack and Ireland was in grave danger.

'Summon all the champions of Ireland at once,'
ordered the High King. 'We must hold a Council of War.'

Famous heroes from far and wide soon arrived at
the castle. Skilled craftsmen and women came too,
who could work all sorts of magic to help in the battle.
Then the High King commanded the Council to begin...

Meanwhile, a latecomer strode up to the castle gates.

'Who goes there?' roared the gatekeeper through his
spyhole. He didn't know what to make of the stranger.
The young man had no battle scars, but he was dressed
as a warrior king.

'My name is Lug,' the stranger shouted back. 'I want to join the Council.'

'Only people who are the master of their craft have been allowed to join the Council,' replied the gatekeeper. 'What do you do?'

'I'm a blacksmith,' said Lug.

'The best blacksmith in Ireland is already here,' said the gatekeeper smugly.

'I am also a carpenter,' continued Lug.

'The best carpenter in Ireland is already here,' retorted the gatekeeper.

'And I'm a fantastic poet and storyteller,' added Lug.

'The best poet and storyteller in Ireland is already here,' snapped the gatekeeper, becoming annoyed. 'Go away.'

Lug didn't give up. He tried healer, magician, musician... and each time, the gatekeeper turned him down.

Lug would not be beaten.

'Tara may already have a master for each of these crafts, but I am master of them all!' he insisted.

'All right, all right!' growled the gatekeeper at last. 'Let me see what the High King has to say.'

The gatekeeper disappeared and Lug waited patiently. After a long time, Lug heard the sound of bolts being drawn back and heavy keys being turned in huge locks.

Then the gates creaked open.

'It's your lucky day,' the gatekeeper told Lug. 'The High King says that if you can beat his players in a game of fidchell, then you can join the Council.'

Fidchell was a difficult board game, a bit like chess. The best fidchell players in all Ireland were inside Tara, but Lug played like no one had ever seen before. He moved his pieces around the board like lightning. He even invented a brand new move. Lug beat every challenger.

The High King was delighted by Lug's skill, but Tara's champion strongman, Ogma, was outraged by the boldness of this stranger. Ogma decided to teach Lug a lesson. He bent down and wrenched an enormous flagstone from the floor. The onlookers gasped. It had taken eighty oxen to drag each flagstone into place! Ogma strained and heaved the flagstone out of the Great Hall and across the courtyard and set it down with an echoing thud outside the castle gates.

'Perhaps Lug would like to put it back?' Ogma smirked, dripping with sweat.

Without a word, Lug picked up the huge stone as easily as if it were a pancake. Then with a flick of his wrist, he tossed it over the castle's towering walls. The flagstone landed in exactly the right place.

While the War Council members muttered to each other in amazement, Lug began to play his harp and sing. Everyone fell silent. Lug's magical music and beautiful melodies filled every man and woman with new energy, ideas and courage. When the wonderful harmonies died away, everyone leapt to their feet and clapped.

'From now on you shall be known as The Master of Masters,' the High King announced. 'You are so gifted that I want you to be the leader of my Council of War.'

Lug went to work on the war plans straight away. He instructed Tara's magicians to turn the trees and rocks into extra warriors to fight the enemy. Then they made Ireland's twelve lakes and twelve rivers invisible, so the giants would find nothing to drink. The magicians also conjured up magic spears which never missed their target.

Then the battle began. Lug and the heroes of Ireland fought long and hard. Finally Lug came face to face with a terrifying giant chief called Balor. This giant had an evil eye that instantly killed anyone it glanced upon. This was great for enemies, but not so good for friends, so Balor usually kept his eyelid shut by weighting it down with a special brass ring. The ring was so heavy that it took four giants to lift it. When Balor saw Lug on the battlefield, he ordered his evil eye to be opened.

As the giants struggled to lift the ring, Lug pulled out his slingshot and fired a magic stone. The stone knocked Balor's evil eye right out of his head and sent it spinning through the air, killing every giant its gaze passed over.

So many giants were slain by Balor's evil eye that their army never recovered. The Irish chased them out of the kingdom forever and the victorious Lug ruled as a mighty king for forty glorious years. What happened to the hero after that remains a mystery. Some say that he died by drowning. Others believe that he became a god and that he has watched over Ireland ever since.

# THE HOUND OF CULAN

Setanta was an extraordinary boy. He began to walk before most children his age could even crawl. He learned to read before most other toddlers could speak. As a five-year-old, he was taller, faster and stronger than boys of eight and nine. When adults spoke to him, he would listen carefully and reply wisely.

Nobody was really very surprised that Setanta was so unusual. His mother, the beautiful Dechtire, had been magically whisked away on her wedding night. She had disappeared without a trace for nearly a year. When she had finally returned, it was with a baby boy. This was Setanta. People later found out that Dechtire had been taken to the land of the gods and that Setanta's father was Lug – the legendary hero who had earned the name The Master of Masters.

Dechtire's brother was an Irish king – Conchobar, King of Ulster. As soon as Setanta learned who his uncle was, he longed to go to the king's court and be trained as a great warrior. So at the age of only seven years old, Setanta ran away from home. He strode boldly all the way to the king's castle.

'My mother is Princess Dechtire,' Setanta announced proudly. 'I want you to give me a prince's education.'

The astonished king could see that Setanta had all the makings of a mighty warrior, so he agreed to let the boy stay. Over the next few years Setanta was taught fighting skills and wisdom by Ulster's greatest heroes and poets.

By the time Setanta was twelve, he had become well known in Ulster as the top goal scorer on the castle hurley team. The other players of the rough stick and ball game were grown men, but the young boy outshone them all. Setanta played with the spirit of a wild animal and the skill of a magician. No one could stop him when he raced down the pitch with the hurley ball bobbing on his stick, and if anyone was in the way when he hit the ball – well, they saw stars for weeks.

Setanta was in the middle of a game one day when the king pulled up in his chariot.

'Come here at once, Setanta!' the king bellowed. 'It's time to go to the feast of Culan the blacksmith.'

Setanta's face fell in disappointment.

'Just ten more minutes, uncle?' he pleaded. 'I just want to score one more goal and then I will come.'

The king tried not to smile.

'Very well,' he said, in his best stern voice.

'But don't be late.'

Of course, Setanta's ten extra minutes stretched into twenty... and then thirty... and by the time the boy hurried to Culan the blacksmith's hall, everyone was making merry inside with the doors firmly locked. In all the fun, everyone had forgotten about Setanta. Culan the blacksmith had even set his bloodthirsty guard dog roaming around outside to scare off intruders.

As soon as the beast sniffed the young boy approaching, he bared his razor-sharp teeth and began to growl. With a howl of hunger, he sprang forward to attack. Luckily, Setanta still had his hurley stick and ball. Quick as a flash, he threw the ball as hard as he could at the snarling dog. It went straight into the brute's mouth and stuck in his throat. While the startled dog coughed and choked, Setanta seized him by the back legs and bashed him up and down until he was dead.

The commotion brought everyone rushing out of the hall.

'My guard dog!' gasped Culan the blacksmith. 'How will I protect my hall now?'

Setanta suddenly felt very guilty.

'Don't worry,' he said with a grin. 'I will be your guard dog until you find a new one.'

From that moment on, Setanta was known as Cuchulain, which means The Hound of Culan. News quickly spread far and wide about the strange, young warrior who guarded the blacksmith's hall. Most bandits and thieves didn't dare to attack. Those who did soon regretted it when they found themselves fiercely attacked and then chased away.

Eventually, Culan the blacksmith no longer needed his human hound. The king, who was impressed with Cuchulain's fighting skills, made the young man a real warrior. Cuchulain's dream had finally come true!

Cuchulain's first job was to fight off three brothers who had been terrorizing the people of Ulster with violence and black magic. Many warriors had challenged the brothers, but they had all been hacked to pieces.

When Cuchulain went out to meet the brothers, he had a strange light in his eyes. Then a terrible change came upon him. His skeleton swivelled inside his skin, one eye bulged out of his head, sparks poured from his mouth and his body hissed with heat. He killed the terrified brothers in a matter of minutes.

The victorious young man licked his lips. He had enjoyed his first taste of battle, and he was to savour many more.

Cuchulain spent his life defeating monsters and magic spells, knights and nobles, kings and queens, until he became the most feared and admired man in the whole of Ireland.

Whenever Cuchulain went into battle, his fighting spirit took him over and he was seized with a fiery frenzy. It was strange and terrible to see.

Finally Cuchulain died a glorious death. He was surrounded on the battlefield, totally outnumbered by enemies. He lashed himself to a tall stone so he wouldn't fall if he was wounded. Ireland's greatest ever warrior died on his feet, fighting to the very last.

# A Tale of Trouble

Fedlimid was a storyteller at the court of King Conchobar of Ulster. He was very excited for two reasons. Firstly, his wife was about to give birth to their first child. Secondly, the king had honoured Fedlimid by coming to stay with him. The king had brought along his famous band of warriors called the Red Branch. There they all were, the finest nobles in Ulster, enjoying a splendid feast in Fedlimid's hall. The storyteller thought things couldn't be better. Until, that is, a servant came with news that Fedlimid's child had at last been born. It was a baby girl!

At once, everyone cheered and stamped and clapped. They slapped Fedlimid on the back and clinked their goblets together. Only Cathbad the Druid wasn't smiling. He had the gift of seeing into the future and he didn't like what he saw.

'Today is not a day for celebration, but for mourning,' the Druid declared sadly. 'Fedlimid's new daughter will one day cause the destruction of the Red Branch and the ruin of Ireland. She must be called Deirdre, which means Troubler.'

Fedlimid sank back in his seat, horrorstruck, while several furious Red Branch warriors leapt to their feet.

'Let's kill the baby right now!' one of them shouted, drawing his sword.

Cries of agreement came from all round the hall.

Suddenly the king banged his mighty fist on the table.

'No one will do any such thing! We are here as Fedlimid's guests!' he bellowed.

Reluctantly, the warriors fell silent.

The king decided to take baby Deirdre to a small castle hidden deep in a forest. He instructed a woman called Levarcham to look after the child. He planned to keep Deirdre hidden until she was a grown woman and then marry her himself. The king thought that, as queen, Deirdre would love all Ireland. The Red Branch warriors would protect her because she was the king's wife. That way, Deirdre would not want to harm anyone and no one would want to harm her. Ireland and the Red Branch would be safe.

Tucked away in the forest, Deirdre grew into a happy, gentle young woman. Levarcham loved her like a mother, but Deirdre couldn't help being lonely. The time came when Deirdre began to gaze out of the window and dream of finding a sweetheart.

'I wish I had a husband,' Deirdre sighed one day. 'A husband with skin as white as snow, cheeks as red as blood and hair as black as a raven's feathers.'

'You're describing the king's nephew, Naoise,' Levarcham laughed, before she could stop herself.

From that moment on, Deirdre could think of nothing but Naoise. She pestered Levarcham with questions about him and begged a million times a day to be allowed to meet him. Deirdre grew so unhappy that she became pale and tired and thin. In the end, Levarcham gave in. She invited Naoise secretly to the castle and he and Deirdre fell in love at first sight. Naoise told Deirdre about the prophecy and how the king planned to marry her.

'The only way we can be together is if we run away,' Naoise whispered.

Next morning, when Levarcham went to wake Deirdre, she had gone...

The king was furious when he found out that Deirdre had escaped. He sent out spies to find the lovers. Finally he heard that Deirdre and Naoise were living in a place called Alba, in Scotland. The king ordered the great hero, Fergus, to go and fetch them.

'Fergus, I swear that I will not harm Deirdre and Naoise,' the king told the warrior. 'I just want to talk to them.'

The faithful Fergus never dreamed for one moment that this was a trick. He sailed to Scotland and persuaded Deirdre and Naoise to return to Ireland. The lovers went to stay at the hall of the Red Branch, with Naoise's two brothers and Fergus' sons for company.

That night the happy group was sitting at dinner when suddenly the warriors of the Red Branch burst in and attacked them. Naoise and his two brothers leapt to their feet and defended Deirdre with the courage of lions. They each hacked down more than three hundred of their enemies, but they were hopelessly outnumbered and they stood no chance against the magic spells of Cathbad the Druid. In the end, they were killed.

When Deirdre saw Naoise's body lying lifeless on the ground, she knelt and cradled him in her arms. She sang a beautiful song of sorrow and placed three kisses on his cold lips. Then she collapsed and died of a broken heart.

The triumphant king allowed Deirdre and Naoise to be buried next to each other, but he had a wooden stake hammered into each grave so that no magic could bring them back to life.

'See!' the king crowed to Cathbad the Druid. 'Deirdre is dead, yet Ireland is not in ruins and my Red Branch is as strong as ever.'

In fact it was the start of the prophecy coming true. The Red Branch had brought great shame on themselves by murdering Naoise and his brothers, so fewer and fewer Irish nobles came forward to join them – until eventually there was no Red Branch left at all. Many of the king's people were so horrified by the terrible crime that they began to support another king, splitting Ireland in two.

As for Deirdre and Naoise, two yew trees grew up out of the wooden stakes in their graves. The trees are strong and alive and growing and their branches are entwined, holding each other close forever.

# The Sword in the Stone

As soon as the head bishop woke up, he sighed. It was Christmas morning, but he didn't feel happy. Instead, his heart was heavy with worry. The great King Pendragon of the Britons had died without leaving a son to take his place. It was up to the bishop to decide who would be the new king, but he simply couldn't think of anyone who would make as good a king as Pendragon. Besides, no matter who he chose, the other lords would be jealous. They probably wouldn't even accept his decision. They might even start fighting each other over it!

The bishop shook his head gravely and swung his feet out of bed. He padded across the cold stone floor to the window. Maybe some deep breaths of fresh winter air would clear his brain and help him come up with the answer! The bishop peered out over the snowy city. His sleepy eyes suddenly opened wide. There in the courtyard of the great church was a huge stone. On top of it was a blacksmith's anvil with a mighty sword stuck in the middle. The bishop was certain that it hadn't been there the night before!

The bishop hurriedly wrapped himself in a cloak and dashed out into the cold. Nervously, he touched the stone. It felt hard and icy enough to be real. He ran his fingers down the sword blade. *Ow!* It was certainly sharp enough to be real. Then the bishop noticed words carved around the middle of the anvil. They read: *Whoever pulls out this sword is the rightful king of the Britons*. The bishop's face lit up.

'It's a miracle!' he gasped.

Later that morning, the great church filled with the finest lords and ladies in the land. There was a glint of excitement in the bishop's eye as he said the Christmas service. Then he made his special announcement.

'There is a sword in a stone in the courtyard,' the bishop cried. 'Whoever pulls it out will be king!'

Everyone gasped in amazement. For a moment they were all rooted to the spot, then the lords suddenly leapt up and dashed for the door. There was a mad scramble as they raced to be the first to reach the stone.

After a lot of pushing and shoving, one lord managed to clamber up and grab hold of the sword.

'It's mine!' he yelled and yanked as hard as he could. The sword didn't budge.

The crowd fell silent and the disappointed lord tried again.

He planted his feet firmly and gripped the sword with both hands. He let out a roar and pulled with all his might.

The sword didn't shift an inch.

Another lord jumped up and pushed the first lord out of the way. This lord's muscles were bigger than the first and he roared louder, too, but the sword still did not move. One by one, every single lord in the city took their turn. And one by one, they all slunk away, shaking their heads.

By the time the sun set, the sword was still firmly in the stone. The bishop spent another night worrying that the Britons still had no king.

Nearly a week later, it was time for the New Year's Eve jousting competition. Every year, knights came from far and wide to ride against each other and show their bravery. One of the knights who came to the event every year was Sir Ector. This year, Sir Ector was even more excited than usual about travelling to the capital city. It wasn't because he wanted to try to pull the sword from the stone. Sir Ector lived so far away that he hadn't even heard of the strange challenge. No, this year was special because Sir Ector was taking his eldest son, Sir Kay, to fight in the jousting competition for the first time. His youngest son, Arthur, was going along too, as Sir Kay's squire.

The two knights and their squire took three days to reach the outskirts of the capital city. They looked a splendid sight as they rode along on their sleek, proud horses. Sir Ector and Sir Kay wore their newest, most highly polished armour. Arthur carried a colourful banner that flapped gaily in the wind.

Suddenly, as they drew near to the jousting fields, Sir Kay realized something terrible.

'My sword is gone!' he cried, turning very pale. 'I must have left it at our lodging house last night.'

'Don't worry, I'll go back and fetch it,' said Arthur, eager to help his brother.

He turned his horse round at once and galloped back down the road. There wasn't a moment to lose. When he reached the lodging house he jumped down from his horse and frantically searched the rooms. To his horror, Sir Kay's sword was nowhere to be found. The weapon had vanished.

Arthur's head drooped as he rode back toward the city. He was a useless squire! Kay wouldn't be able to take part in the competitions without a weapon. Arthur was thinking how to break the bad news to his brother, when he rode past the courtyard where the strange sword was still stuck in the stone.

'Whoa!' Arthur cried, yanking on his horse's reins. His worried face broke into a beam.

'Everyone's at the joust,' he said to himself. 'I'm sure no one will miss that sword if I just borrow it for a while.'

Arthur jumped down and sprinted across the snow. Quick as a flash, he pulled the sword out of the stone as easily as a knife slides through butter. Arthur gazed at the golden hilt and gleaming blade.

*Kay will be sure to win with this*, he thought with glee. *It's the finest weapon I've ever seen!*

Arthur galloped to the jousting fields as fast as he could and, breathless and grinning, handed the magnificent sword to his older brother.

By now, Sir Ector and Sir Kay had heard all about the mysterious anvil from the other knights at the jousting competition. As soon Sir Kay felt the wonderful new sword in his hands, he knew it must be the weapon that everyone was talking about.

'Father, look! I must be the rightful king of the Britons!' Kay yelled in delight.

As Kay brandished the mighty weapon above his head, an excited crowd began to gather.

Sir Ector looked sternly at his eldest son.

'Where did you get this, Kay?' he said in a firm, low voice. 'Did you pull it from the stone yourself?'

The young knight lowered his eyes.

'No, father,' he admitted. 'Arthur brought it to me.'

Without a word, Sir Ector led Arthur back to the churchyard.

'Put the sword back where you found it, Arthur,' Sir Ector said gently.

They were surrounded by a huge crowd. The news had spread like wildfire and everyone had dashed to the church courtyard. In front of all the silent, staring eyes, Arthur thrust the sword back into the anvil. Sir Ector tried as hard as he could to pull it free. Then Sir Kay did his best. But it was no good.

'Show us how you did it, son,' Sir Ector said.

Once again, Arthur wrapped his fingers around the hilt and the blade slipped effortlessly out of the anvil.

The crowd began to whoop and cheer with joy as they realized they were looking at their new king.

'I have something I must tell you,' Sir Ector whispered, hugging Arthur. There were tears of pride in his eyes. 'You are not my own flesh and blood. You were brought to me as a tiny baby by Merlin, the king's magician. Now I realize that you must be the son of Pendragon himself.

But I promise that I have always loved you as my own son and I always will.'

Soon afterwards, Arthur was crowned king of the Britons. The bravest, noblest knights in all the land hurried to join his court at Camelot. They went on many bold adventures together, battling for good against evil. Stories spread far and wide of their brave deeds. Arthur's knights soon became known as the Knights of the Round Table and King Arthur himself became the most famous of all Celtic heroes.

# THE DEATH OF KING ARTHUR

Merlin the magician was deeply worried. King Arthur had married the beautiful Lady Guinevere. They were very happy together, but Merlin knew that Arthur's best friend, Sir Lancelot, loved Guinevere too. The wise old enchanter was sure that trouble and sorrow lay ahead...

Merlin was right. The king's sworn enemy, Mordred, saw a chance to take Arthur's place as king. Gleefully, Mordred spread rumours that Lancelot and Guinevere were meeting behind Arthur's back. The furious king believed the lies and the couple fled the country. Arthur set off after them, intending to fight Lancelot.

Mordred's evil plan was working. With Arthur away, he seized the throne. Arthur dashed back and a bloody battle took place. At last Mordred lay dead, but Arthur himself was badly wounded and close to death.

As the king lay bleeding, he handed his sword to the faithful Sir Bedivere. This sword wasn't the one Arthur had pulled from the stone long ago. It was an even more powerful weapon called Excalibur. Excalibur had been mysteriously given to Arthur by the Lady of the Lake. The king knew that it was time to give the sword back.

45

'Take Excalibur to the lake and throw it in,' Arthur ordered Sir Bedivere.

With tears in his eyes, the knight staggered down to the water's edge. A heavy mist hung over the lake, shimmering in the moonlight. Sir Bedivere looked at Arthur's beloved sword. Soon this sword would be all that was left of the king. Instead of throwing Excalibur into the water, the knight hid it and hurried back.

'What did you see?' Arthur croaked weakly.

'Nothing but ripples on the water,' Sir Bedivere replied.

The king knew that the knight wasn't telling the truth.

'Go and do as I asked,' he gently commanded.

Sir Bedivere returned to the lake with a heavy heart. He found the precious sword and raised it high, ready to hurl it. Then he stopped. He simply couldn't bring himself to do it. Again Sir Bedivere hid Excalibur and raced back to the dying king.

'What did you see?' Arthur gasped weakly.

'Nothing but the waves lapping the shore,' Sir Bedivere replied.

'My friend, don't let me down after all these years,' Arthur whispered.

Hanging his head in shame, Sir Bedivere went back to the lake and took Excalibur from the hiding place.

With a roar of anguish, he flung the mighty weapon high into the air. Before the gleaming sword could splash into the water, a hand came up out of the lake and caught it. The hand brandished Excalibur three times and then pulled it underwater.

When the knight told Arthur what had happened, the king smiled and closed his eyes. Then Sir Bedivere carried Arthur to the water's edge. A dark, funeral boat glided silently out of the mist and Sir Bedivere lifted Arthur aboard. The sorrowing knight raised his hand in farewell and the greatest ever Celtic king was borne away to the magic island of Avalon. Some people say that Arthur is there to this day, ready to return when his people need him.

# INDEX